I0116105

THE PRESIDENT

The Man the World Needs Now

ANTHONY MWANGI

Crony Trading LTD

This book is dedicated to
leaders who refuse to inherit collapse
and choose instead to steward continuity.

To presidents, governors, prime ministers, legislators, judges, and executives
who understand that authority is not self-generated
but entrusted.

To those who know that power without righteousness
destabilises systems, and vision without discipline bankrupts nations.

To the Daniels of this generation, men and women formed in quiet integrity,
trained in wisdom,
steady under pressure,
unmoved by corruption,
and fluent in both heaven's counsel and earth's realities.

May this work serve as a compass,
a governance framework,
and a reminder that the highest office
is ultimately accountable to truth.

For such a time as this.

"Blessed is the nation whose God is the LORD;
and the people whom he hath chosen for his own inheritance."
— Psalm 33:12 (KJV)

"He changeth the times and the seasons:
he removeth kings, and setteth up kings:
he giveth wisdom unto the wise, and knowledge to them that
know understanding."
— Daniel 2:21 (KJV)

A presidency aligned with heaven does not merely manage power; it interprets the moment, stewards the season, and governs with eternal accountability.

SABBATH FIRE

CONTENTS

FOREWORD

A Mandate for the Hour

Leadership is the ultimate leverage point of history.

When leadership is aligned, nations compound value.
When it is misaligned, nations bleed slowly: often invisibly, until collapse looks sudden but was inevitable.

This book enters the global conversation at a critical inflection point. Across continents, the presidency has been reduced to optics, brand management, and short-term wins. Power is abundant. Wisdom is scarce. Information is everywhere. Understanding is rare.

The President — The Man the World Needs Now is not a critique; it is a recalibration.

It reframes leadership as a trust, not a trophy. As stewardship, not self-expression. As alignment with higher order, not merely ideological dominance. In corporate terms, this work functions as a **governance reset,** returning executive authority to its original design parameters.

Daniel stands at the centre of this framework not as a religious symbol, but as a proven operating model. He governed across empires, cultures, and crises without losing moral clarity or institutional relevance. His leadership scaled. His integrity endured. His influence outlasted regimes.

That alone demands attention.

This book does something rare: it integrates **spiritual intelligence with executive competence**. It speaks to presidents, prime ministers, policymakers, advisors, and emerging leaders who understand that nations are ecosystems and that unseen variables often determine visible outcomes.

The chapters ahead address real-world pressures: economic volatility, moral drift, security threats, succession risk, and cultural fragmentation. Yet they refuse to treat symptoms in isolation. Instead, they propose a leadership architecture rooted in timeless principles, tested under pressure, and applicable at scale.

The tone is sober because the moment demands sobriety.
The vision is hopeful because alignment always produces renewal.
The counsel is firm because leadership without truth is unsustainable.

This is not idealism. It is **strategic realism anchored in eternal order**.

If read with humility, this book will challenge assumptions.
If applied with discipline, it will strengthen institutions.
If ignored, the consequences are already familiar to history.

The world does not need another personality in office. It needs a **pattern restored**.

This foreword is an invitation to leaders willing to govern beyond ego, beyond cycles, beyond fear, and to step into a presidency that answers not only to voters, but to conscience, justice, and time itself.

The moment is now.
The responsibility is heavy.
The opportunity is unprecedented.

Proceed with clarity.

INTRODUCTION

The modern presidency sits at the intersection of pressure, perception, and power. Markets watch. Media scrutinises. Citizens demand. History records. Yet beneath the visible mechanics of office lies an invisible battlefield where the real outcomes of nations are decided.

This book opens with a simple but disruptive premise: **every presidency governs more than people—it governs atmospheres**.

Daniel understood this before political science named it. He operated inside imperial systems without becoming owned by them. He advised kings without flattering them. He interpreted crises without panic. His authority did not rise from charisma or conquest, but from **clarity of alignment**. Heaven endorsed his stewardship because he refused to confuse power with ownership.

In today's operating environment, presidents inherit volatile economies, fragmented cultures, weaponised information, and fatigued populations. The instinctive response is control; more regulation, more force, more messaging. Yet control without coherence accelerates decay. What nations require is **moral gravity**: leadership that stabilises simply by being rightly ordered.

This Introduction sets the strategic context for the chapters ahead. We will examine the presidency not as a ceremonial role, nor as an executive monopoly, but as a **custodial office;** responsible for preserving national identity, stewarding resources, and navigating unseen pressures that influence visible outcomes.

You will encounter themes that feel ancient yet urgent:

- Power as stewardship, not entitlement

- Law as a moral signal, not merely enforcement

- Economy as trust management, not extraction

- Foreign policy as both diplomatic and spiritual engagement

- Crisis as revelation, not interruption

The goal is not nostalgia. It is **future-readiness**.

This book does not argue that presidents must preach. It asserts something more demanding: **they must perceive**. Discernment is the competitive advantage of righteous governance. Without it, even well-intentioned leaders become reactive, fragmented, and eventually compromised.

Throughout history, when leadership lost its moral compass, nations outsourced meaning to ideology, entertainment, or force. When leadership regained alignment, cultures healed, and prosperity followed. The pattern is consistent. The variables are not.

The chapters ahead map a presidency that can withstand corruption, interpret complexity, and partner with heaven without abandoning constitutional order. This is not idealism. It is **governance architecture** tested across time.

The world is not waiting for a stronger president. It is waiting for a **clearer one**.

What follows is an invitation to reimagine leadership; not as dominance, but as discernment; not as survival, but as stewardship; not as ambition, but as assignment.

The Daniel President is not a myth of the past. He is the blueprint for what must rise next.

PREFACE

This book was not written to critique power. It was written to **reframe it**.

Across history, presidencies have been engineered for efficiency, defended by force, and justified by ideology; yet nations continue to fracture. The missing variable has never been intelligence, resources, or systems. It has been **alignment**.

The world is not suffering from a leadership shortage. It is suffering from a **governance vacuum at the spiritual level**.

Daniel stands as the benchmark. Not because he sought office, but because heaven trusted him with influence. He did not campaign. He was positioned. He did not dominate systems. He **interpreted them**. Through successive empires, shifting ideologies, and existential crises, Daniel proved a non-negotiable truth: when leadership is aligned with divine order, stability becomes sustainable.

This book advances a forward-looking thesis: **the presidency is not merely a political office; it is a stewardship of times, atmospheres, and national identity**. Every policy decision registers beyond economics. Every crisis response echoes in the unseen realm. Every leader either partners with order or negotiates with chaos.

The chapters that follow do not offer a theory detached from reality. They present an **operating framework;** one that integrates spiritual intelligence with institutional accountability; moral clarity with executive competence; prophetic insight with constitutional restraint.

This is not a religious manifesto. It is a **governance model**.

Here, righteousness is not rhetoric; it is infrastructure. Integrity is not optional; it is national security. Prophecy is not prediction; it is **direction**. And leadership is not measured by tenure, but by testimony.

If the world is to stabilise, it will not be through louder voices or stronger weapons. It will be through leaders who can stand in complexity without surrendering truth; who can interpret seasons without being intoxicated by power; who understand that authority is borrowed, time-bound, and answerable.

This book is written for presidents yet unborn, for systems preparing succession, and for citizens discerning what leadership must become.

The Daniel President is not an ideal. He is a **necessity**.

What follows is not aspiration. It is alignment.

PROLOGUE

When Kings Lose Their Way

The Executive Crisis of a Generation

Power is loud, but purpose is quiet.
And somewhere between those two sounds, the world has lost its leaders.

Nations are drifting like unmanned ships.
Institutions groan under invisible pressure.
Governments scramble for solutions while their moral compasses spin without a North.

You can feel it in the streets.
You can hear it in the news cycle.
You can discern it in the atmosphere.

A global leadership haemorrhage.

And when kings lose their way,
people bleed.
Truth bends.
Justice starves.
Destiny stalls.

But heaven does not panic.
Heaven never improvises.
Heaven responds with a pattern.

A pattern older than empires.
A pattern carved into Scripture.

A pattern tested in the furnace of nations.

Daniel — the first president.

A statesman who carried intelligence from another realm.
A public officer whose integrity could not be purchased.
A thinker whose mind navigated kingdoms the way sailors navigate seas.
A man whose competence was so rare that emperors leaned on his insight more than their armies.

He rose without campaigning.
He influenced without manipulating.
He governed without corruption.

Daniel was not appointed by consensus.
He was appointed by **excellence, revelation, and spiritual accuracy** — the three pillars that heaven still requires from leaders today.

His life was not merely a testimony.
It was a **template**.
A living executive blueprint for leadership in times of crisis.

And this is the moment when the world needs that blueprint again.

For governments are facing pressures they were never designed to carry:

- fragmented societies

- collapsing moral structures

- economic volatility

- digital warfare

- institutional distrust

- the loss of truth as a national asset

Modern presidents walk into office carrying storms, not platforms.

But heaven has already spoken.
Heaven has already modelled the solution.
Heaven has already revealed **the man the world needs now**:

A president with Daniel's clarity.
Daniel's wisdom.
Daniel's integrity.
Daniel's discipline.
Daniel's spiritual intelligence.
Daniel's courage to stand alone when systems fail.
Daniel's ability to translate God's mind into public policy.

This book is not political theory.
It is not leadership philosophy.
It is not a critique of governments.

It is a **prophetic leadership architecture;** a throne-room brief for presidents, kings, governors, CEOs, ministers, and those awakening to their national assignment.

Because God has not abandoned nations.
He is raising men and women who carry the same ancient excellence, the same unwavering righteousness, the same calm authority that made Daniel a stabilising force in Babylon.

When the earth cries for leadership, heaven answers with a man.

And that man is not defined by office… but by obedience.

Not by position… but by purity.

Not by popularity… but by spiritual intelligence.

This is the President the world needs now. And Daniel is the blueprint.

CHAPTER 1

The Prototype President: Daniel

Core Insight: Daniel is heaven's gold standard for public office.

When heaven needs a steward for nations, it does not send politicians. It sends a man forged in the discipline of the Spirit, seasoned by trial, fluent in wisdom, and anchored in character. Daniel is not an ancient curiosity; he is an executive prototype — the durable chassis upon which modern presidential leadership must be rebuilt.

The Spirit of Excellence — the Presidential Baseline

Excellence is non-negotiable. Daniel's life teaches that a leader's first credential is competence carried with humility. He entered a foreign court as an underling and left as indispensable because he refused mediocrity. Excellence is not performance for applause; it is relentless inner discipline; study, self-mastery, preparation — that converts potential into presidential capital.

Corporate application: calibrate KPIs (character, competence, credibility) before campaigning. Institutionalise daily disciplines that sustain national performance metrics: ritual prayer/strategy sessions, doctrinal literacy, and an ethic of excellence in small things that scale to national outcomes.

Integrity Under Pressure — the Lion's Den Test

Pressure reveals architecture. When laws conspired against Daniel, his integrity did not bend; it activated. The lion's den is the metaphor for every public crisis that tests a leader's principle under legal and political fire. Integrity in office protects institutions; compromise corrupts them.

Executive playbook: build legal walls around conscience; transparent decision trails, immutable oversight, and a personal code of conduct that survives personal cost. Train a leadership inner circle to resist expedience and to make sacrificial choices that preserve national soul.

Strategic Wisdom — the Dream Interpreter

Daniel interpreted dreams because he habitually translated heaven into policy. He moved information from realm to realm: revelation into counsel, vision into strategy. Modern presidents must do the same: convert prophetic insight and data intelligence into pragmatic policy.

Modern protocol: create an Office of Strategic Revelation; a fusion cell that marries prophetic discernment with intelligence analysis, scenario planning, and policy simulation. Use prophetic forecasting as an early-warning system, then test it against empirical models.

Nation-Scale Influence Without Corruption

Daniel held office across shifting empires and never let power become an agent of personal enrichment. Influence that endures is influence that refrains from exploitation. A president who uses the office as a storefront for self collapses institutions into patronage.

Governance mechanics: decentralise authority; rotate appointments through meritocratic pipelines; enforce strict conflict-of-interest statutes; publish open ledgers. Make public service a covenant, not a commodity.

Prophetic Intelligence — Knowing Times, Seasons, and Futures

Daniel lived by seasons. He read empires like weather charts. Prophetic intelligence is not vague mysticism; it is situational acumen combined with spiritual sensitivity. Leaders who master seasons decide not only how to survive but how to shape history.

Operationalising prophecy: mandate season-readings: quarterly prophetic briefings integrated with economic forecasts, security assessments, and cultural trend reports. Teach leaders to move with rhythm; when to sow, when to harvest, when to reform, when to rest.

The Presidential Soul — Humility + Spiritual Clarity

At the heart of Daniel's leadership was a soul trained in humility. He refused the adornments of pride. He prayed, he fasted, he consulted heaven before the court. The presidential soul is a disciplined centre: humility that listens; clarity that decides.

Leadership culture: institute rites of humility for office-holders; mandatory periods of retreat, spiritual accountability partners, and public acts that reorient power toward service.

Modern Presidential Alignment — From Blueprint to Boardroom

Translating Daniel's archetype into twenty-first-century governance requires structures, processes, and culture shifts.

- **Decision-making pipelines:** map clear authority flows. Move from ad-hoc decrees to playbooks that scale across ministries. Adopt "fast lanes" for crisis and "slow lanes" for structural reform.

- **Crisis response culture:** train for cognitive calm. Simulate media, cyber, and moral crises until response becomes reflexive and principled.

- **Multi-national diplomacy:** operate from covenant, not just contract. Negotiate with the posture of a witness — truthfully, generously, strategically.

- **High-stakes negotiation:** deploy prophetic leverage: convene spiritual counsel before diplomatic strategy; convert moral capital into diplomatic capital.

- **Policy forecasting:** merge prophetic briefings with econometric models. Make policy contingent on both revealed trajectory and data-driven projection.

- **Anti-corruption architecture:** harden institutions with transparency tech, whistleblower sanctuaries, rotating audits, and prosecutorial independence.

Each of these is a governance vector. When aligned with the Danielic soul, they form a gravitational field that corrects falling nations.

Biblical Counsel for the Executive

The Bible does not offer only stories; it prescribes frameworks. *Proverbs 4* teaches the pursuit of wisdom as protection. *Psalm 25* models public humility and instruction-seeking before God. *Daniel 6* demonstrates how law, prayer, and conviction coordinate to preserve a leader's testimony under siege.

Read these texts not as devotional accessories but as operational manuals: make them daily briefings, not just nightly readings.

Practical Playbook — Seven Immediate Actions

1. **Institute a daily "Stillness Briefing"** — 20 minutes of prayer and prophetic listening before the war-room convenes.

2. **Create a Leadership Integrity Charter** — publicly signed,

permanently posted, legally enforceable.

3. **Stand up a Strategic Revelation Cell** — staffed by historians, economists, and spiritual counsellors.

4. **Publish a National Integrity Ledger** — real-time financial transparency for all senior offices.

5. **Mandate Season-Readings** — quarterly prophetic/economic fusion reports for cabinet pivoting.

6. **Simulate the Lion's Den** — annual legal and ethical stress tests for the executive team.

7. **Train Succession Cadres** — leadership academies built on character, competence, and covenant.

Closing Charge (A Brief Commissioning)

O God of wisdom, give to those who govern the Excellence spirit like onto Daniel: clarity where confusion swarms, courage where compromise waits, and steadfast humility that values truth above favour. Raise men and women who will carry excellence as armour, integrity as law, and prophetic intelligence as counsel. Instruct them to translate heaven's mind into public policy; let their offices become altars of justice and stewardship.

CHAPTER 2

The President Must First Be a Prophet

If he cannot hear God, he cannot lead nations.

T his is the immutable law of righteous governance. Every true president, from heaven's vantage point, begins not with a cabinet, not with an oath, but with an altar. The prophetic is not a title. It is a posture.
It is not charisma. It is calibration. It is the executive ability to read what others only feel, and to interpret what others only fear. When the president loses the prophetic ear, he becomes a technician of crises, not a transformer of nations. Daniel teaches us that spiritual intelligence is the first infrastructure of leadership.

1. Hearing the Word — The President's Antenna

Before Daniel advised kings, he aligned with heaven. He read scrolls. He prayed. He fasted. He listened until wisdom crystallised.

Modern presidents read reports.
Prophetic presidents read realities.

The prophetic leader hears:

- The warning behind the numbers

- The counsel inside the chaos

- The pattern beneath the politics

- The command embedded in Scripture

This is strategic governance at spiritual altitude.

2. Interpreting Mysteries — Turning Data Into Revelation

Daniel didn't guess his way through crises. He interpreted. He converted mystery into a mandate. He brought **clarity** where others brought **panic**.

Today's presidency is flooded with:

- Economic puzzles

- Geopolitical knots

- Emerging technologies

- Spiritual decay

- Demographic revolutions

A prophetic president sees not only the *what*, but the *why*.
Not only the trendline, but the timeline. Not only the threat, but the throne that governs it.

3. Discerning Threats — Seeing the Invisible Enemy

Daniel saw the spirit behind the empire, the intent behind the decree, the danger hidden inside the routine.

A prophetic president discerns:

- Ideological infiltration

- Cyber warfare signals

- Moral corrosion spreading through culture

- Foreign influence disguised as partnership

- Early signs of civil unrest

- Hidden corruption nodes within the system

Threats become visible when the leader's spirit is awake.

4. Seeing Beyond Political Optics — Leading from the Throne Room

Politics is noisy. The prophetic is steady.
Public opinion is emotional. The prophetic is eternal.

A president shaped by the Spirit:

- Leads from the mind of God

- Refuses to be trapped by polls

- Breaks free from party cages

- Makes decisions aligned with purpose, not popularity

This is governance with spine, governance with vision, governance with covenant clarity.

MODERN APPLICATION — How the Prophetic Converts Into Governance

• Intelligence Briefings → Prophetic Discernment

A normal president reads the briefing. A prophetic president reads the handwriting behind the briefing.

• Cybersecurity → Watching the Digital Gates

Every digital system is a gate. Every gate is a moral and spiritual portal. The prophetic president understands breaches before they happen.

• Global Risk Mapping → Seeing Future Storms

Daniel mapped empires before they rose. Prophetic leaders map events before they erupt. This is proactive stewardship.

• Social Moral Decline Indicators → Reading the Soul of a Nation

When morality erodes, economies follow.
When families collapse, governments shake.
When truth is lost, power becomes violent.
The prophetic president reads these signs like a shepherd watching the weather.

BIBLICAL COUNSEL — The Prophet-President's Architecture

- **Jeremiah 1** — The call to uproot, tear down, build, and plant: presidential authority birthed in prophetic identity.

- **Isaiah 11** — The Sevenfold Spirit as the executive operating system: wisdom, understanding, counsel, might, knowledge, and fear of the Lord.

- **Revelation 19:10** — The testimony of Jesus as the spirit of prophecy: the true foundation of righteous governance.

CLOSING PRESIDENTIAL CHARGE — "Stand in the Counsel of God"

Mr. President,
Before you sit at the Resolute Desk, sit in the secret place.

Before you sign laws, let God write His law on your heart.

Before you command armies, let the Spirit command you.

Before you speak to nations, listen to heaven.

Lead not from anxiety, but from alignment. Not from ambition, but from assignment.

Your mandate is not merely to govern a people, but to steward destiny. You are called to be a voice in a generation drowning in noise. A lighthouse when nations lose their maps. A pattern when rulers collapse into confusion.

As Daniel stood in Babylon, so must you stand in this age; unbending, discerning, illuminated.

This is your charge:
Govern prophetically.
Lead righteously.
Stand courageously.
Listen continually.

PRACTICAL PROPHETIC DISCIPLINES FOR LEADERS

These practices are not mystical; they are managerial. They form the operational rhythm of a president who leads with God's mind.

1. Morning Scripture Calibration

One chapter of Scripture before one briefing.
Set the spiritual compass before the political compass.

2. The Daniel Hour — Daily 3x Alignment

Morning. Noon. Evening.
Short pauses to:

- Reset perspective

- Listen inwardly

- Seek wisdom

- Ask for clarity

This keeps the leader's spirit sharp.

3. Weekly Intelligence + Intercession Review

Bring together:

- Spiritual advisors

- Intelligence experts

- Policy analysts

Ask:
"What is heaven highlighting this week?"

4. Strategic Silence

One day a month with no media, no meetings, no noise.
This is not escape—this is renewal.
Leaders think clearer when they breathe deeper.

5. Accountability Circle

Daniel had Shadrach, Meshach, and Abednego.
A president needs:

- Moral challengers

- Strategic thinkers

- Honest truth-tellers

This prevents drift.

6. Annual National Fast & Reflection

A president turns the nation's heart back to God not by speeches alone, but by example.

CHAPTER 3

*Executive Presence: The
Spirit of Excellence*

Daniel distinguished himself — not by charisma, but by competence.

T here are two kinds of leaders: The ones who shine, and the ones who rise. Daniel rose. Not because he performed, but because he **excelled**. Heaven endorsed him. Earth recognised him. Systems shifted to accommodate him. His excellence wasn't polish; it was presence; a spiritual steadiness that made kings tremble and empires listen. Excellence, in heaven's dictionary, is not perfection. It is alignment. It is the capacity to bring divine order into human systems without losing purity, clarity, or conviction. Daniel becomes the executive template God still uses when appointing leaders to reform nations.

1. Uncompromising Standards — The Presidential Benchmark

Daniel refused the king's meat.
That single decision calibrated his entire future.

Excellence starts with refusal.
The president the world needs must know what he will never

touch:

- Corruption
- Bribery
- Immorality
- Compromise for votes
- Popularity-driven leadership
- Secret pacts with darkness

Uncompromising standards build unshakable credibility.

When the president bends on small things, he breaks on great things.

2. Daily Disciplines — The Hidden Machinery of Greatness

Daniel prayed three times a day; not as a ritual, but as a rhythm.

Daily disciplines create:

- Mental clarity
- Executive stamina
- Moral accuracy
- Strategic foresight
- Emotional maturity

A president cannot rely on inspiration.
He must rely on **routine**.

The world is governed by what a leader repeats:

- Early rising
- Scripture meditation

- Briefing review
- Decision audits
- Physical conditioning
- Solitude thinking

Excellence is built one discipline at a time.

3. Purity of Inner Life — Integrity as National Infrastructure

Daniel's inner world was clean. He had no skeletons in the closet, no hidden alliances, no moral fractures.

The inner life of a president eventually becomes the outer life of a nation.

When a president's heart is divided:

- Policy becomes confused
- Advisors become manipulative
- Departments become corrupt
- Citizens become cynical

Purity is not private; it is national security.

A president governs atmospheres before he governs people.

4. Resilience Under Pressure — The Lion's Den Leadership Model

The lion's den wasn't punishment.
It was proof.

Daniel's greatness was authenticated under pressure.
Nations need presidents who:

- Stay calm when markets collapse
- Lead firmly in foreign aggression

- Hold moral ground during cultural upheaval

- See clearly when surrounded by political predators

Pressure reveals the president's true substance: Not fear. Not bravado. But resilience; steady, spiritual, unbending.

MODERN APPLICATION — Excellence in Governance

1. Cabinet Leadership — Culture at the Top Sets the Tone Below

A president must build:

- A morally aligned cabinet

- A competence-driven executive team

- A truth-telling advisory circle

- A corruption-resistant culture

Daniel influenced three kings; today's president must influence every department.

Excellence at the top produces integrity in the ranks.

2. Economic Policy — Stewardship, Not Showmanship

Excellence in economics requires:

- Stewarding national productivity

- Eliminating waste

- Creating sustainable growth

- Ensuring just scales and fair measures

- Protecting the poor without empowering dependency

Daniel understood that kingdoms rise or fall based on the stewardship of resources.

A modern president must govern budgets with biblical restraint and prophetic foresight.

3. Foreign Policy — Diplomacy With Discernment

Excellence in foreign policy requires understanding both:

- The geopolitics of nations
- The spiritual identities of nations

Daniel read empires through prophecy, not polling.

A president must:

- Discern intentions
- Manage alliances
- Prevent ideological infiltration
- Build peace without surrendering sovereignty

The spirit of excellence produces diplomacy anchored in truth, not fear.

4. Healthcare, Education, Workforce Culture — The Human Capital Mandate

A nation is only as healthy as the people who carry it.

The spirit of excellence compels a president to:

- Strengthen healthcare quality
- Elevate educational standards
- Build ethical workplaces
- Promote innovation
- Protect family structures

• Ensure workers are valued, not exploited

Excellence touches human life at every layer.

BIBLICAL COUNSEL

Proverbs 22:29 — "Seest thou a man diligent in his business? he shall stand before kings."
2 Timothy 2:15 — "Study to shew thyself approved unto God... rightly dividing the word of truth."

Daniel lived both verses.
A president must embody them.

CLOSING PROPHETIC IMPACT STATEMENT

Excellence is not optional for a president; it is oxygen.
It is the fragrance of a life aligned with God's order.
It is the signature that distinguishes rulers shaped by heaven from rulers shaped by ambition.

CHAPTER 4

Decision-Making Under Fire

W hen the furnace of leadership burns hottest, ordinary men melt. Daniel did not. He stood; calm, clear, unshaken while empires convulsed around him. He led under assassination plots, regime shifts, suspicious advisers, and hostile spiritual climates.

Yet nothing bent him.

Nothing diluted him.

Nothing intimidated him.

This chapter decodes the leadership technology behind Daniel's unbreakable judgment.

THE REALITY OF PRESIDENTIAL FIRE

Every president faces the same crucible Daniel endured, only modernised:

- Media storms designed to distort truth

- Public backlash amplified by digital mobs

- International conflicts where missteps cost lives

- Constitutional pressures engineered by political adversaries

- A nation divided, angry, polarized, impatient

- Advisory tables filled with mixed motives

- Hidden spiritual warfare behind public policy battles

The presidency is not a job. It is a furnace. And only the leader who governs from a higher realm survives it without losing himself.

Daniel teaches us that the heat does not destroy the righteous leader — it reveals him.

SECTION 1 — MEDIA STORMS: When the World Is Watching

Modern presidents stand before global media machines that thrive on drama.

Daniel faced:

- False accusations

- Public scandal

- Weaponised narratives

He responded not with panic, but with **presence**.

A prophetic president must:

- Anchor facts before responding

- Refuse emotional reactions

- Communicate clarity without fuelling chaos

- Keep dignity even when under attack

- Let truth outlive noise

Noise is temporary. Truth is eternal. Excellence is visible.

A president with Daniel's spirit outlasts every manufactured storm.

SECTION 2 — PUBLIC BACKLASH: Leading Amid Anger

A nation's mood can change in a day. Crowds react emotionally before they think rationally.

Daniel stayed steady while Babylon swung between:

- Reverence

- Jealous fury

- Political manipulation

A president must:

- Listen without being led by outrage

- Respond without bowing to pressure

- Maintain ethical north when polls fall

- Keep the nation's soul above the nation's noise

Public backlash tests identity. Those who don't know who they are drown in opinion.

SECTION 3 — INTERNATIONAL CONFLICTS: Navigating the Global Stage

Daniel interpreted the rise and fall of empires before they happened. He saw geopolitical shifts before kings felt the tremors.

A president must:

- Read foreign intent accurately

- Resist emotional alliances

- Prevent ideological infiltration

- Understand spiritual identities of nations

- Use diplomacy without losing sovereignty

- Choose peace without compromising justice

This is not traditional foreign policy.
This is prophetic statesmanship.

SECTION 4 — CONSTITUTIONAL PRESSURES: When Law Becomes a Weapon

Daniel 6 is the blueprint. His enemies weaponised law to trap a righteous man. They did not argue morality. They engineered legality. The same happens today.

A president must discern:

- Hidden motives in legislation

- Legal language crafted to corner him

- Judicial traps disguised as reforms

- Policies designed to sabotage righteous governance

Daniel's mastery of legal frameworks saved his life.
Presidents need the same mastery to save their administrations.

SECTION 5 — POLARISED CITIZENS: Governing a Divided Nation

Daniel served kings who ruled empires filled with:

- Captives

- Foreigners

- Idolaters

- Divided cultures

- Opposing religious systems

He governed without favouritism.
He applied wisdom without partiality.

A modern president must:

- Speak to the whole nation, not just the base

- Build unity without sacrificing truth

- Enforce justice without bias

- Heal divisions without creating new ones

- Discern cultural spirits behind national tensions

Polarisation is a battlefield. The president is the bridge, or the accelerant. Daniel shows us how to be the bridge.

HEAVEN'S STRATEGY FOR DECISION-MAKING UNDER FIRE

1. Stillness Before God — The Leader's Quiet Command Centre

Before reacting, Daniel **stilled** his soul. He let God interpret the moment before he interpreted it.

Stillness gives:

- Accuracy under pressure

- Clarity amid noise

- Restraint when provoked

- Wisdom for complexity

- Courage for unpopular decisions

Stillness is not inactivity. It is strategic spiritual positioning.

2. Daniel 6 Legal Mastery — Understanding Systems Before They Trap You

Daniel's enemies crafted a law about prayer. He discerned the trap immediately.

The president must:

- Understand his constitution
- Master national legislative frameworks
- Read between the lines of policy proposals
- Identify who benefits from every clause
- Track which spiritual powers influence which laws

A leader who lacks legal understanding becomes a victim of legal manipulation.

3. Courage as a Non-Negotiable — The Backbone of Governance

Courage is not a feeling. It is a decision to stay aligned with the truth when fear has the louder megaphone.

Daniel stood when others bowed. He prayed when others hid. He remained visible when an attack was inevitable.

A president must:

- Take unpopular stands
- Confront corruption
- Challenge hostile powers
- Act decisively in crisis
- Choose righteousness over reelection

Courage is the executive spine of greatness.

4. Truth Before Optics — Heaven's Leadership Protocol

Daniel did not polish the truth for acceptance. He delivered it raw, accurate, and unfiltered.

Truth outlasts optics. Truth dismantles manipulation.

Truth exposes hidden agendas. Truth guides destiny.

Optics manage perception.

Truth shapes nations.

A president who chooses truth becomes immovable.

CLOSING PROPHETIC FRAME

A president is never judged by calm days. He is defined by the furnace.

Daniel did not survive Babylon. He mastered it.

Heaven is raising leaders who can:

- Stand in storms
- Govern in crises
- Decide with clarity
- Lead without fear
- Think above pressure
- Rule without compromise

Leadership under fire does not crush the righteous; it forges them.

CHAPTER 5

The President and the Economy

D aniel managed Babylon's economic engines through wisdom. Every empire has a beating heart. It is not the palace. Not the military. Not the Senate. It is **the economy**; the bloodstream of national life. When the economy shakes, everything shakes. When it stabilises, hope rises. Daniel understood this. Joseph embodied it. Both governed economies under hostile empires, yet both rose to the highest administrative seat because they carried **God's economic intelligence.** The modern president must now do the same: govern markets with vision, money with morality, and systems with righteousness.

SECTION 1 — HEAVEN'S VIEW OF NATIONAL ECONOMICS

Biblically, the economy is not about wealth. It is about **order, stewardship, justice, and covenant alignment.**

Money reveals:

- the heart of leadership

- the soul of a nation

- the values driving the culture

• the hidden loyalties of the people

When a nation's economy collapses, its spiritual alignment has already collapsed long before.

Daniel and Joseph governed from heaven's perspective:

• wealth must serve a purpose

• resources must serve justice

• systems must serve people

• leaders must serve God

This is the prophetic architecture of economic stability.

SECTION 2 — MODERN APPLICATION: ECONOMIC BATTLEFIELDS EVERY PRESIDENT FACES

1. Inflation — The Silent National Erosion

Inflation does not shout; it whispers. It eats savings, wages, stability, and hope.

A president with Daniel's wisdom must:

• stabilize currency

• limit unjust price manipulation

• protect vulnerable families

• evaluate global market dependencies

• ensure honest weights and measures

Inflation exposed is manageable. Inflation ignored becomes national trauma.

2. Trade Systems — The Flow of Nations

Behind every trade agreement is a spiritual agreement.

Behind every tariff war is a power struggle.

A righteous president must:

- negotiate without surrendering sovereignty

- avoid exploitative partnerships

- strengthen domestic industries

- diversify supply chains

- protect national identity while engaging global markets

Trade is not just commerce; it is covenantal alignment.
Daniel would warn kings not to trade righteousness for revenue.

3. Food Security — The Joseph Mandate

Joseph understood that food systems determine survival.
Nations fall when food fails.

A president must:

- protect agricultural infrastructure

- build resilient storage systems

- invest in technology-driven farming

- prevent foreign control of food supply

- foresee famine cycles and prepare

Food is not merely provision.
Food is prophecy.
Who controls food controls the future.

4. National Debt — The Invisible Chain

Debt is modern bondage.

A president with biblical clarity must:

- avoid predatory international lenders
- reduce dependency cycles
- strengthen internal revenue integrity
- curb overspending
- build long-term fiscal sustainability

Scripture warns that *"the borrower is servant to the lender."*
A nation in excessive debt is not sovereign; it is managed.

5. Corporate Partnerships — Wisdom in High Places

Daniel served kings without becoming their puppet.

A modern president must:

- work with corporations without bowing to them
- empower innovation without selling the nation's soul
- ensure ethical governance in business
- break monopolistic power
- create transparency in procurement

A president who cannot stand firm before CEOs cannot stand firm before nations.

6. Greed-Proof Systems — The Heart of Righteous Economics

Daniel could not be bought. Joseph could not be bribed.
Jesus exposed economic hypocrisy with surgical precision.

A president must build systems that:

- prevent corruption before it begins

- audit money flow relentlessly

- protect whistleblowers

- enforce integrity in public offices

- dismantle elite capture and shadow networks

Greed collapses nations faster than war.
Excellence in economics begins by eliminating the spiritual cancer called corruption.

SECTION 3 — BIBLICAL COUNSEL FOR NATIONAL ECONOMIC LEADERSHIP

1. Joseph's Economic Model

Joseph teaches:

- save in years of plenty

- anticipate long-term cycles

- stabilise nations through foresight

- manage resources prophetically

- structure fair distribution

- build trust between the government and citizens

Joseph was not just interpreting dreams; he was designing economies.

2. Proverbs on Stewardship

Proverbs gives the president:

- principles of fair trade

- warnings against debt

- ethics of honest scales

- wisdom for strategic planning
- instructions for generosity and justice

These are the economic laws of heaven.

3. Jesus' Teachings on Justice

Christ confronted:

- exploitative systems
- dishonest leadership
- hypocritical wealth
- unjust taxation
- economic oppression of the poor

Jesus did not avoid economics — He purified it.

Justice is the backbone of every godly economy.

PROPHETIC SUMMARY: THE PRESIDENT AS ECONOMIC PRIEST

A president is more than a policymaker.
He is the steward of national destiny.
Every budget is a moral document.
Every policy is a reflection of spiritual alignment.
Every economic decision shapes generations.

Daniel managed wealth without worshiping it.
Joseph governed resources without hoarding them.
Jesus redefined value according to the kingdom.

When a president carries that spirit, nations flourish.
When he does not, economies groan.

CHAPTER 6

The President as Moral Compass

L aws shape morality. Morality shapes destiny.
Before a president commands armies, before he drafts budgets, before he negotiates treaties: he must **guard the soul of the nation.**

Every law passed is a sermon.
Every policy is a moral compass.
Every reform is a declaration of what the nation believes.

A president who abandons morality abandons the nation's future. A president who upholds righteousness becomes the unseen architect of national destiny.

This is the realm Daniel mastered. He did not merely interpret dreams; he interpreted **right and wrong** for empires trapped in moral confusion.

SECTION 1 — THE PRESIDENT AS THE NATION'S ETHICAL NORTH

Righteousness is more than virtue. It is governance.

When a leader upholds righteousness:

- the land stabilises
- the people flourish
- corruption weakens
- culture aligns with truth
- justice gains weight
- heaven partners with nations

When a leader tolerates wickedness:

- darkness multiplies
- families disintegrate
- crime escalates
- courts become compromised
- truth decays
- national identity fractures

Morality is not a private issue. It is the president's highest public duty.

SECTION 2 — MODERN APPLICATION: BATTLEFRONTS OF NATIONAL MORALITY

1. Sexual Ethics — The Foundation of National Wholeness

Sexual confusion births generational confusion. Immorality fractures souls, families, and entire cultural frameworks.

A president must:

- protect children from corrupt ideologies
- uphold biological truth
- safeguard national identity from moral distortion

- legislate protections against exploitation and abuse

- preserve the sanctity of marriage and covenant

When sexual ethics collapse, society loses spiritual oxygen.

2. Family Policy — The First Government

Before kingdoms existed, families existed. Before kings existed, fathers existed. Family is God's original governance system.

A president must:

- strengthen family structures

- uphold parental rights

- fund family-centred support systems

- protect motherhood and fatherhood

- design policies that make righteousness sustainable

If the home crumbles, the nation crumbles.

3. Education Truth Standards — Guarding the Minds of a Generation

Education is discipleship. Every curriculum shapes worldview. Every classroom forms identity.

A president must:

- safeguard curriculum purity

- ensure truth is not replaced with ideology

- promote literacy of Scripture, history, and reality

- prevent moral indoctrination

- elevate academic excellence over political propaganda

Whoever controls education controls tomorrow.

4. Crime and Justice — The Moral Pulse of a Nation

Criminal justice is not about punishment. It is about righteousness restoring order.

A president must:

- ensure fair courts
- uphold impartial justice
- protect communities from lawlessness
- deepen police integrity
- dismantle systems that enable violence

Justice reveals the moral temperature of leadership.

5. Protection of the Poor — The Test Heaven Never Ignores

God measures nations by how they treat the vulnerable.

Daniel served systems full of inequality and still became a defender of the weak.

A president must:

- guard the widow, the orphan, the stranger
- build transparent welfare structures
- prevent exploitation of labour
- ensure economic access and fairness
- create pathways out of poverty without political manipulation

Where the poor are crushed, heaven withdraws.

6. National Righteousness — The DNA of Sustainable Destiny

A righteous president steers the nation toward blessing. An unrighteous president steers it toward judgment.

Righteousness gives:

- stability
- clarity
- unity
- longevity
- national healing

Wickedness produces:

- decay
- chaos
- confusion
- instability
- spiritual drought

A president's moral posture becomes the nation's spiritual climate.

SECTION 3 — BIBLICAL COUNSEL FOR A PRESIDENTIAL MORAL COMPASS

Psalm 15 — The Qualifications for Holy Leadership

God requires leaders who:

- walk uprightly
- speak truth

- reject bribery

- refuse slander

- honour the fearful of the Lord

This is the ethical backbone of divine governance.

Micah 6:8 — **Heaven's Three-Fold Executive Standard**

"Do justly. Love mercy. Walk humbly with God."

Justice — the president's public posture
Mercy — the president's social posture
Humility — the president's spiritual posture

This is the moral mission statement of righteous leadership.

Deuteronomy 16:20 — **The President's Constitutional Command**

"That which is altogether just shalt thou follow..."

Justice is not an option.
It is a command.
It is a covenant.
It is a national survival strategy.

Righteousness is security.
Justice is national armour.
Truth is national oxygen.

PROPHETIC CHARGE: THE PRESIDENT AS THE NATION'S CONSCIENCE

A president must rise beyond politics.
Beyond popularity.
Beyond public pressure.

He must:

- defend morality even when culture rebels

- legislate righteousness even when elites resist

- stand for truth even when institutions collapse

- protect families even when ideologies rage

He is the flame-holder.
The conscience-bearer.
The moral anchor in stormy times.

If he fails here, everything else collapses.
If he stands here, the nation can weather any storm.

CHAPTER 7

Foreign Policy And The Principalities

When Nations Negotiate With Thrones, They Cannot See

A president does not merely sit across from other presidents. He sits across from principalities, powers, and ancient dominions that have shaped nations for centuries.

Daniel knew this first. He met the "Prince of Persia." And in that moment, diplomacy shifted from political calculus to **spiritual warfare disguised as foreign policy.**

This—right here—is the battlefield no president can afford to ignore.

1. The Unseen Infrastructure of Nations

Every border is also a spiritual boundary.
Every treaty has an invisible counterpart.
Every government hosts either:

- **righteous thrones that uphold justice**, or

- **dark principalities that manipulate power, wealth, war, and culture.**

Daniel's world was governed by kings, but ruled by spiritual atmospheres.

Babylon's brilliance was powered by sorcery.
Persia's empire was influenced by a ruling spirit.
Greece had a principality of intellect and philosophy.
Rome carried the principality of conquest.

Modern nations are no different.

2. Modern Application — The Invisible Stakeholders of Foreign Policy

• Territorial Spirits

Some nations carry ancient altars:

- violence

- corruption

- idolatry

- oppression

- witchcraft

- bloodshed

A president must discern what sits on a nation's throne
before signing anything.

• International Alliances

Some alliances strengthen sovereignty. Others entangle nations with spiritual debts.

A president must ask:

"What spirit rules the nations we are aligning with?"

Diplomacy is not just policy; it is spiritual arithmetic.

- **Peace Frameworks**

Peace is not the absence of war; it is the **presence of righteous governance**.

Daniel brought peace to kingdoms because he brought the counsel of God.

Presidents who carry prophetic intelligence establish peace that endures cycles, ideologies, and elections.

- **War Thresholds**

Sometimes the war is political.
Sometimes economic.
Sometimes cultural.
Manytimes **demonic**.

A president must know when to stand down and when heaven commands a stand-up.

- **Prophetic Diplomacy**

This is where Daniel shinned:

- accurate interpretation of global transitions

- reading the spiritual climate behind political movements

- translating heaven's intelligence into earthly policy

- navigating kings with prophetic restraint and strategic brilliance

Prophetic diplomacy is the merger of:
Revelation + Intelligence + Timing + Wisdom.

3. Heaven's Counsel for Presidents Who Confront Principalities

1. Understand Atmospheres

Foreign policy must begin with atmospheric discernment.

The president must ask: *What spirit governs this nation's capital?*

2. Do Not Negotiate From Fear

Principalities can smell intimidation. They pressure weak leaders into treaties that enslave nations.

Daniel stood with unbroken calm because heaven stood with him.

3. Build Righteous Infrastructure at Home

A nation that is spiritually corrupt internally cannot stand against foreign principalities externally.

Holiness is not a religious ideal; it is **national defence infrastructure**.

4. Establish Prophetic Advisory Pipelines

A president needs:

- intercessors

- prophetic analysts

- spiritual intelligence officers

- watchmen who discern times and seasons

Not as a religious circle, but as a national security protocol.

5. Keep the Throne of God Above the Throne of Man

If a president bows to God, no principality can enslave his administration.

4. Biblical Counsel

Daniel 10

The gold standard for understanding how national governance interacts with spiritual powers.

Ephesians 6

The constitutional framework of spiritual conflict: The real war is not against nations, but against ancient hierarchies of darkness.

Presidential Charge — Standing Before Thrones Seen and Unseen

President, you do not negotiate alone. You sit at tables where angels and principalities lean in to listen.

Lead with clean hands. Discern the atmosphere.
Read the invisible signatures beneath treaties.
Align your nation with righteousness, and heaven will reinforce your borders.
Stand in the authority of the Spirit, and no dominion of darkness will intimidate you.

CHAPTER 8

*Transparency, Accountability &
Presidential Purity Corruption*

When the Throne Is Clean, the Nation Breathes Again

C orruption is the silent assassin of kingdoms.
It erodes trust, drains national strength, and invites
judgment.
It is decay disguised as strategy.
It is darkness wearing a suit.
A president may reform the economy, fix foreign policy, and
master diplomacy, but if purity is compromised, **the entire nation
becomes infected.**

Daniel stood in a palace dripping with bribery, seduction, idolatry,
and political conspiracy. Yet he emerged without stain. This is the
presidential standard of heaven.

1. Presidential Purity Is National Infrastructure

Purity is not a moral accessory. It is a **governance architecture**.

When the president is clean:

- justice flows,

- budgets stabilise,

- institutions strengthen,

- corruption loses air,

- darkness loses home,

- and the nation exhales.

When the president is impure:

- dark networks multiply,

- spiritual gates open,

- demonic economies flourish,

- and the soul of the nation fragments.

This chapter is not about moralism. It is about kingdom mechanics.

2. Modern Application — Integrity Systems of a Righteous President

External enemies do not destroy the modern presidency, but by compromise internal ecosystems.

• Budget Transparency

No hidden accounts.
No shadow allocations.
No coded "special projects."
Budgets are spiritual statements: they reveal **the nation's god**.

Daniel administered empires with mathematical clarity.
A president who hides nothing stands on unshakable ground.

• Ethical Audits

Not just financial audits; **ethical audits** of institutions, ministries, and partnerships.

Daniel's righteousness disinfected entire systems.
Heaven endorses presidencies that confront internal rot.

• Anti-Bribery Law

A nation is only as righteous as the agreements made in its corridors.

Bribery is not a crime; it is a **spiritual covenant with Mammon**.

A president must break it publicly, legally, and culturally.

• Removal of Rogue Influences

Every administration attracts:

- power brokers,
- ideological saboteurs,
- spiritual infiltrators,
- financial opportunists.

Daniel survived by refusing to sit at Babylon's table.
A president must discern who carries influence and who carries **infection**.

• Purity of the Inner Circle

The strength of a presidency depends on the holiness of its "first ring."

If the inner circle is compromised, the nation is compromised.

The president's gatekeepers must be fire-tested in integrity, loyalty, and truth.

3. Heaven's Blueprint for Presidential Accountability

Daniel's model is radical:

- no dual loyalties

- no hidden vices

- no double speech

- no private agreements

- no moral fractures

This purity produced:

- clarity under pressure

- boldness before kings

- accuracy in interpretation

- angelic engagement

- national favour

- long-term trust

Purity is not perfection; it is alignment with heaven.

4. Psalm 101 — The Presidential Psalm

Psalm 101 is the original executive oath.
It is the throne-room leadership code.
Every line is a governance standard.

"I will behave myself wisely in a perfect way."
→ Presidential strategy must be anchored in moral intelligence.

"I will walk within my house with a perfect heart."
→ Private purity is national security.

"I will set no wicked thing before mine eyes."
→ No corruption. No compromise. No immoral alliances.

"A froward heart shall depart from me."
→ Remove toxic influence immediately.

"Mine eyes shall be upon the faithful of the land."
→ Appoint clean, loyal, principled leaders.

"He that worketh deceit shall not dwell within my house."
→ Zero tolerance policy toward manipulation.

Psalm 101 is not poetry; it is **executive policy** handed down from the throne of God.

5. Prophetic Implications for National Leadership

When a president embraces purity:

- angels guard the administration

- corruption collapses internally

- prophetic clarity sharpens

- the atmosphere of governance shifts

- the nation becomes spiritually breathable

- heaven partners with national development

Purity is not optional. It is presidential oxygen.

Presidential Charge — The Integrity Mandate

President, your purity is the nation's shield.
Your transparency is the nation's backbone.
Your accountability is the nation's longevity.
Stand clean. Stand clear. Stand unbribed.
If your heart remains undefiled, your administration will stand unshaken.
Lead with integrity, and heaven will underwrite your governance.
This is the way kings rule without decay, and nations rise without

ANTHONY MWANGI

sorrow.

CHAPTER 9

The President and National Identity

When a Nation Forgets Itself, It Forfeits Its Future

I dentity is not culture.
Identity is not history.
Identity is not geography. Identity is calling.
A nation is born when heaven speaks.
A nation dies when it forgets that voice.

A nation without identity becomes a wandering spirit; moving, but not advancing; busy, but not becoming; prosperous, but not purposeful.

Presidents do not merely govern land. They govern **memory**, **meaning**, and **mission**.

And when Daniel rose in Babylon, one of his quiet assignments was this: **preserve the identity of God's people in a foreign empire.**

He refused assimilation.
He refused dilution.
He refused the erasure of who he was.

Daniel carried identity like a sealed scroll. He stood in foreign courts without becoming a foreign man.

This is the presidential grace needed today.

1. National Identity Is a Prophetic Asset

Identity is not nostalgia; it is strategy.

Nations collapse when:

- their story is rewritten,

- their heroes are erased,

- their spiritual heritage is mocked,

- their youth lose self-worth,

- their culture is traded for trends.

A nation that forgets its divine script will adopt a script written by its enemies.

Daniel shows us that identity is the oxygen of destiny.

2. Modern Application — The President as Guardian of National Soul

• Cultural Restoration

A president must restore what corruption, colonisation, secularism, and moral erosion have fractured.

Every culture holds:

- wisdom deposits,

- generational codes,

- spiritual memory,

- national resilience.

The president must retrieve these fragments and rebuild the national soul.

- **Language Protection**

Language is identity's vault.

When language dies:

- worldview collapses,
- memory weakens,
- spiritual nuance disappears,
- unity cracks.

Daniel kept his Hebrew consciousness alive even while mastering the language of Babylon.

A modern president must guard national languages as sacred repositories of destiny.

- **Spiritual Heritage**

Every nation has a spiritual root structure.

If the root is cut:

- the fruit becomes foreign.
- the culture becomes hollow.
- the people become wanderers.

A president must honour the nation's spiritual foundations and remove ideologies that erode moral conscience.

- **Civic Unity**

Unity is not sameness. Unity is direction.

A president must align tribes, clans, races, regions, and classes under a shared mission.

Division is never political; it is spiritual.

Whoever fractures unity fractures destiny.

- **Youth Identity Renewal**

The youth are the nation's prophecy.

If their identity is confused:

- crime rises,
- depression spreads,
- productivity collapses,
- spiritual clarity disappears.

A president must rebuild the identity ecosystem of the young:

- purpose education
- patriotic mentorship
- spiritual literacy
- community responsibility
- national ethos formation

A nation lives or dies in the identity of its youth.

3. The Prophetic View — Nations Have Scrolls

Every nation has a scroll (**Deut. 32**). A prophetic storyline written before time. A divine purpose assigned to its people.

When leaders govern without reading the national scroll, they lead blindfolded.

Daniel understood Babylon's scroll, Medo-Persia's scroll, and Israel's scroll.

This made him the rarest type of leader: a man who knew what heaven intended for every nation he served.

A president must learn to discern:

- national assignment
- national gifts
- national wounds
- national enemies
- national angels
- national future

Identity is not an emotion; it is a **prophetic map**.

4. Biblical Counsel — Deut. 32 & Psalm 33:12

Deuteronomy 32

A national memory book. God recounts how He formed, carried, preserved, and aligned a nation.
It is a warning: **Nations perish when they forget the Rock that begat them.**

Psalm 33:12

"Blessed is the nation whose God is the LORD."
Identity is anchored not in ethnicity, but in allegiance to God. A nation blessed is a nation aligned.

5. Presidential Charge — Guard the National Soul

President, the nation you lead is not a crowd; it is a calling.
Protect its language.
Restore its culture.
Revive its spiritual memory.
Lift its youth into purpose.
Guard its unity like a flame in the wind.

If you protect the nation's identity, heaven will protect its destiny.
For a nation that remembers its God will never be forgotten by heaven.

CHAPTER 10

Crisis Management: Fires,
Floods, Pandemics, Wars

Leadership in the Hour When Nations Shake

A president is never truly revealed in peace. He is revealed in crisis. Storms expose foundations. Pressure reveals purity. Chaos uncovers competence. And panic unmasks pretenders.

Daniel lived inside the pressure chambers of empires:

- collapsing kingdoms,

- violent transitions,

- assassination plots,

- economic unravelling,

- spiritual warfare at national scale.

Yet he stood with a serenity that felt spiritual, because it was **spirit-born**.

Heaven designed Daniel as the template for crisis leadership. And in a generation groaning under global volatility, this template becomes non-negotiable.

1. Crisis Is Not an Event — It Is a Revealer of the Leader

Daniel never waited for calm before executing wisdom. He carried internal stillness into external storms.

This is the presidential paradox:
Leaders do not wait for peace — they manufacture it.

Daniel governed through:

- sudden regime collapses,

- mass hysteria,

- prophetic warnings,

- looming invasions,

- impossible political pressures.

His calm was his weapon.
His clarity was his shield.
His accuracy was his authority.

2. Modern Application — Crisis Management in a Turbulent Age

The crises of today are more complex than ancient wars.
They are multidimensional: political, environmental, digital, biological, spiritual.

A modern president must lead through **layered chaos**.

▪ Climate Disasters

Wildfires, floods, droughts, cyclones; these are not random environmental malfunctions. They are signals of creation groaning (*Romans 8*).
A president must build:

THE PRESIDENT — THE MAN THE WORLD NEEDS NOW

- rapid response systems

- resilient infrastructure

- climate-aware urban planning

- national readiness drills

- disaster relief networks

- food and water security pipelines

Daniel understood seasons and signs.
A president must do the same.

- **Health Emergencies**

Pandemics collapse:

- hospitals

- economies

- supply chains

- public trust

- mental health

A president must lead with:

- transparency, not panic

- science, not superstition

- coordination, not confusion

- prayer, not presumption

Daniel fasted and prayed for national healing.
A wise president uses both divine counsel and medical intelligence.

- **Political Coups**

Power vacuums arise when:

- corruption matures,

- institutions weaken,

- security agencies fracture,

- tribal tensions spike.

Daniel survived the overthrow of kings because his loyalty was to God first, nation second, office third.

This is the hierarchy of an incorruptible president.

- **Digital Attacks**

Cyber warfare is the new battlefield.
It can:

- shut down banks

- cripple hospitals

- collapse communication

- trigger financial panic

- manipulate elections

- hijack national identity

A president must build:

- cyber defence command centres

- data sovereignty protocols

- digital threat intelligence

- cross-border cyber alliances

Daniel interpreted encrypted mysteries.
A modern president must protect digital mysteries.

- **Mass Migrations**

Forced migration tests:

- compassion

- security

- economics

- culture

- international reputation

Daniel knew what exile felt like.
He governed with empathy toward displaced people because he had been one.

A president must balance mercy with border strategy and wisdom with humanity.

3. Heaven's Blueprint — The Daniel Approach to Crisis

Daniel's crisis response can be summarised in four executive pillars:

1. Stillness Before God (*Daniel 2*)

Before Daniel spoke to kings, he listened to heaven.
In crisis, reaction is the enemy; stillness is strategy.

2. Accuracy Under Pressure

Daniel never guessed. He sought the mind of God until clarity emerged.
Presidents collapse under pressure when they make decisions in fear. Accuracy is birthed in communion.

3. Legal Mastery (*Daniel 6*)

Daniel understood the laws of the realm and used them with precision.

Crisis leadership requires:

- constitutional awareness

- policy intelligence

- legal foresight

Ignorance is costly in the hour of emergency.

4. Courage as the Executive Backbone

Courage is not emotional bravery. It is spiritual positioning.
Daniel stood unshaken when lions roared.
Presidents must stand unshaken when nations panic.

4. Biblical Counsel — *Isaiah 43 & Psalm 46*

Isaiah 43 — The Crisis Manual

> *"When thou passest through the waters...*
> *when thou walkest through the fire..."*

God does not promise *avoidance* of crisis.
He promises *presence* in crisis.
This is the presidential comfort:
You are not alone in the fire.

Psalm 46 — The Leadership Psalm

> *"God is our refuge and strength,*
> *a very present help in trouble."*

Though the earth shakes and mountains crumble, the leader anchored in God becomes immovable.

This psalm is not poetry; it is the posture of crisis-proof

governance.

5. Presidential Charge — Lead the Fire, Don't Fear It

President, crisis does not weaken you. It reveals you.
Stand inside the storm with Daniel's stillness.
Lead with accuracy, not emotion.
Move with courage, not fear.
Establish systems that anticipate chaos and strategies that outlive panic.
If God walks with you in the fire, no flood, no plague, no war, no digital storm can overthrow your leadership.

CHAPTER 11

Leadership Succession &
Legacy Architecture

Daniel Outlasted Kings — Because Legacy Outlives Tenure

Legacy is not the memory of a leader.
Legacy is the continuation of his obedience.
Daniel did not merely survive transitions; he governed them. He watched crowns pass, thrones fall, dynasties collapse, and empires shift, yet he remained the constant voice of God in an inconsistent world.

He understood something every modern president must know: **A leader's greatness is not measured by the era he governs, but by the generation he prepares.**

Legacy is not longevity.
Legacy is testimony; the testimony of wisdom transferred, character imparted, systems secured, and values embedded.

Presidents who fail to build succession condemn a nation to start again every election cycle.
Presidents who build legacy create continuity beyond their lifetime.

1. Legacy in the Danielic Paradigm — Outlasting Empires

Daniel served:

- Nebuchadnezzar

- Belshazzar

- Darius

- Cyrus

Four kings.
Three empires.
One man of God who never lost influence.

How?

Because Daniel was not loyal to power, he was loyal to purpose.

He carried:

- a trans-generational mind,

- a prophetic understanding of timelines,

- a stewardship of national memory,

- a commitment to truth regardless of throne.

Daniel knew that heaven evaluates leaders not by the power they gained but by the people they raised.

This is the architecture every president must build.

2. Modern Application — Succession as National Insurance

Nations decay when leadership collapses. They rise when leadership multiplies.

A president must not merely govern well; he must **ensure governance continues well** after him.

▪ Training the Next Generation

The future is never inherited; it is trained.

A president must:

- mentor emerging national leaders
- invest in young innovators
- cultivate civic responsibility in schools
- build youth empowerment pipelines
- foster leadership integrity in early adulthood

Future leaders do not grow in crisis; they grow in preparation.

▪ Strategic Civil Service

A nation's backbone is not its politicians, but its institutions.

The president must:

- professionalise civil service
- insulate institutions from corruption
- promote merit-based leadership
- develop non-political expertise pipelines
- standardise ethical government training

Daniel himself became an institution. He carried memory, continuity, and competence through empires.

Modern presidents must build systems that cannot be dismantled by the next political wave.

▪ Leadership Academies

Legacy needs structure.

A presidential leadership academy becomes:

- a national leadership engine

- a training ground for future governors, ministers, diplomats

- a sanctuary for values

- a forge for ethics

- a womb for nation-builders

Daniel trained young Hebrew men in Babylon's court without letting Babylon train the God out of them.

That is the model.

• **National Values Curriculum**

Nations are built on values, not elections.

A president must oversee a curriculum that instils:

- truth

- integrity

- patriotism

- justice

- compassion

- spiritual identity

- civic duty

Values must become the nation's immune system.

Legacy is protected by the values the president leaves behind.

3. Prophetic Insight — Legacy Is a Spiritual Structure

Legacy is not sentimental. It is spiritual engineering.

Psalm 78 describes the transmission of national memory:

"that the generation to come might know...
who should arise and declare them to their children."

Legacy is heaven's chain of custody.

Daniel knew that the visions he recorded were not for his time only. They were for **future kings** and **end-time generations**.

He wrote not just to govern Babylon, but to instruct ages yet unborn.

Presidents must think in centuries, not cycles.

4. Biblical Counsel — *Psalm 78 & 2 Timothy 2:2*

Psalm 78 — **The Architecture of Generational Transfer**

This psalm is the blueprint of legacy:

- tell the story,
- teach the truth,
- warn against rebellion,
- establish faith,
- prepare children to lead.

It is a national chain of wisdom, forged in the fear of God, designed to outlive crises, wars, and political shifts.

2 Timothy 2:2 — **The Multiplication Protocol**

"The things thou hast heard...
commit thou to faithful men, who shall be able to teach
others also."

Four generations in one verse.
This is the mathematics of legacy.
This is leadership that cannot die.

5. Presidential Charge — Build What Outlives You

President, your tenure is temporary, but your impact can be eternal.
Raise leaders who can carry the burden with clean hands.
Strengthen institutions that will stand when you are gone.
Write wisdom that will guide rulers yet unborn.
Establish values that cannot be corrupted.
Build architectures that future generations will call blessed.
For true leadership is not measured by your years in office, but by the years your influence remains.

CHAPTER 12

The President and the
Testimony of Jesus Christ

Where the Throne's Witness Becomes the Nation's Compass

A president can command armies, enact laws, sign decrees, and mobilise economies, but only one force possesses the power to align a nation with God's eternal design: **The testimony of Jesus Christ.**

Revelation 19:10 — "For the testimony of Jesus is the spirit of prophecy."

This is not poetic language. It is a constitutional truth for the government of the Spirit.

Prophecy is not prediction.
Prophecy is direction.
Prophecy is architecture.
Prophecy is alignment with the original blueprint written before time.

A president who abandons prophecy drifts.
A president who resists prophecy collapses.
But a president who embraces the testimony of Christ becomes:

- A **witness** to divine order

- A **voice** of righteous government
- A **guardian** of the national destiny
- A **partner** in heaven's unfolding agenda
- A **shepherd** who rules not by fear but by light

The testimony of Jesus is the operating system of righteous governance.

1. The President as Defender of Truth

Truth is not merely a moral standard.
Truth is a spiritual infrastructure.

Lies weaken nations. Truth stabilises nations.

When Jesus stood before Pilate, He said: "To this end was I born… that I should bear witness unto the truth."

A prophetic president understands:

- **Truth is national currency.**
- **Truth is security.**
- **Truth is the shield against corruption, manipulation, and foreign deception.**
- **Truth is the first line of national defence.**

When truth is compromised, governance becomes guesswork and policy becomes witchcraft.
When truth is enthroned, justice flows like water.

2. The President as Guardian of Justice

Justice is not a department; it is a throne.

Psalm 89:14 — "Justice and judgment are the foundation of Thy throne."

A prophetic president enforces:

- Fair courts
- Clean laws
- Balanced judgments

- Equal treatment

But beyond systems, he understands the **spiritual ecology** of justice:

Where injustice lives, demons multiply.
Where justice stands, wickedness flees.

Justice is a spiritual climate tool.

A president aligned with Christ becomes a barrier through which no corrupt power can pass.

3. The President as Shepherd of People

A shepherd doesn't control sheep; he carries vision, protection, and direction.

Jesus said: "I am the good shepherd."

A president in the testimony of Jesus leads from a place of:

- Compassion
- Integrity
- Sacrifice
- Responsibility
- Wisdom

He is not merely a ruler; he is a steward of the people's future.

He does not scatter; he gathers.
He does not devour; he restores.
He does not oppress; he elevates.

Such leadership heals a nation's soul.

4. The President as Witness to Light

Light is revelation.
Light is clarity.
Light is governance.

Isaiah 9 says the government of the Messiah is a government carried by light.

A president aligned with Christ becomes:

- A carrier of national clarity
- A breaker of confusion
- A destroyer of hidden agendas
- A revealer of what threatens destiny

Light exposes darkness.
Light dismantles manipulation.
Light restores moral order.

Nations governed by light become nations of stability and progress.

5. The President as Steward of Times and Seasons

Jesus rebuked the Pharisees:

> *"You can discern the sky, but cannot discern the signs of the times."*

A president led by the testimony of Christ must:

- Read national cycles
- Interpret global shifts
- Discern spiritual storms
- Understand prophetic alignments
- Prepare the nation for the future

This is not mysticism; it is leadership maturity.

Daniel read empires.
Joseph read famine.
Esther read genocide.
David read war seasons.
Isaiah read messianic epochs.

A president's failure to interpret seasons becomes a national tragedy.

A president aligned with Christ sees before others see.

The Presidential Mandate Under Christ's Testimony

To carry the testimony of Jesus is to become:

A prophetic statesman.
A spiritual architect.
A guardian of destiny.
A servant of divine will.
A carrier of national light.

This chapter is the summit because everything rises and falls on this truth:

Nations do not first fall economically — they fall spiritually.
Nations do not first rise politically — they rise spiritually.

And at the centre of that rise is a president aligned with the testimony of Christ.

Prophetic Activation for Presidents and National Leaders

1. **Stand daily at the altar of truth.**
   Let no lie pass through your gates.
2. **Judge righteously.**
   Let justice cleanse the nation like a river of fire.
3. **Walk in light.**
   Let darkness find no resting place in your administration.
4. **Guard the people.**
   Lead with mercy. Govern with clarity. Protect with courage.
5. **Discern the times.**
   Let heaven's calendar shape national strategy.

Presidential Benediction

Let the testimony of Jesus become the constitution of your leadership.

Let prophecy become the intelligence brief of your decisions.

Let truth, justice, mercy, and light become the pillars of your administration.

And may your presidency echo in heaven as one who governed with Christ, ruled with wisdom, and stewarded a nation into its divine destiny.

CHAPTER 13

FULL BOOK I CONCLUSION
The Governance of Light

L eadership is not a theory.
Leadership is not a title.
Leadership is not an office. Leadership is a *witness*.
A nation rises or falls on the spiritual altitude of its leader. Policies shape behaviour. But prophecy shapes destiny. The president is therefore not merely a custodian of government; he is the steward of a nation's covenant.

This book began with Daniel because Daniel understood something modern systems often forget:

Government is spiritual before it is political.
Authority is divine before it is democratic.
Nations are prophetic before they are geographic.

When the president stands in the fear of the LORD:

- Corruption collapses.
- Justice flows.
- Wisdom rises.
- The land rests.
- Destiny aligns.

When the president departs from prophetic counsel:

- Darkness multiplies.
- Chaos accelerates.
- National identity fractures.
- Economic pillars weaken.
- Foreign powers gain leverage.

The testimony of Jesus is not optional for national governance. It is the absolute centre of sustainable authority.

In every chapter, the Spirit has whispered the same truth:

"Rule from the throne, not from the crisis."

- Foreign policy begins in the prayer room.
- Economic stability begins at the altar.
- National identity begins in the covenant.
- Crisis management begins in the waters of *Isaiah 43*.
- Legacy begins in *Psalm 78*.
- Integrity begins in *Psalm 101*.
- Strategy begins in the Spirit of prophecy.

The presidential mantle is not light. It is weighty, but it is not crushing when carried with Jesus.

A righteous president becomes:

- A stabiliser of the nation
- A breaker of demonic influence
- A voice for future generations
- A guardian of the people's dignity
- A steward of heaven's calendar

This is the way of Daniel.
This is the way of Joseph.
This is the way of David.
This is the way of Christ.

And this is now the way of presidents aligned with the Spirit.

Governance is worship.
Leadership is obedience.
Nations are sacred trusts.

May every president who reads these words rise into the realm where decisions become prophecy, and governance becomes glory.

◆ ◆ ◆

THE PRESIDENTIAL OATH
OF THE SPIRIT

A Formal Covenant for Heads of State

"I stand before God, the Judge of all the earth,
and before the people entrusted to my care.
I commit to lead under the testimony of Jesus Christ,
to govern with truth, to defend justice,
and to protect the identity of this nation.

I accept the mantle of stewardship,
the weight of righteous governance,
and the responsibility to discern times and seasons.

I reject corruption, I renounce hidden influences,
and I embrace transparency, accountability, and moral clarity.

I commit to walk in light, to listen to prophetic counsel,

and to rule with wisdom from above.

May my presidency be a witness,
my leadership a testimony,
and my legacy a model of covenant fidelity.

So help me God."

◆ ◆ ◆

THE NATIONAL BLESSING

A Prophetic Benediction Over the Land

"Let this land rise under the canopy of divine order.
Let the Spirit of wisdom govern our decisions.
Let the Spirit of understanding shape our institutions.
Let the Spirit of counsel direct our strategy.
Let the Spirit of might strengthen our defences.
Let the Spirit of knowledge guide our innovation.
Let the Spirit of the fear of the LORD purify our leaders.

Let justice flow.
Let peace reign.
Let corruption crumble.
Let righteousness exalt.
Let truth be the atmosphere we breathe.

May our children inherit a nation anchored in covenant.
May our youth awaken to identity and purpose.
May our elders see the fulfilment of prophecy.
May our gates be secured, our borders defended,
our fields fruitful, our cities restored.

Let the testimony of Jesus Christ
become the architecture of our destiny.

This nation is blessed.
This nation is called.
This nation is aligned."

◆ ◆ ◆

PROPHETIC DECREES FOR LEADERS

High-level executive declarations for those governing under the Spirit

1. Decree of Alignment
"I decree that every decision aligns with the original blueprint of heaven."

2. Decree of Light
"I decree that hidden things are exposed and truth prevails."

3. Decree of Justice
"I decree that corruption collapses under the weight of divine order."

4. Decree of Stability
"I decree national calm, economic resilience, and institutional integrity."

5. Decree of Identity
"I decree that this nation remembers who it is in God's covenant."

6. Decree of Protection
"I decree that foreign manipulation is broken and territorial spirits are displaced."

7. Decree of Vision
"I decree clarity, foresight, and prophetic intelligence for national

strategy."

8. Decree of Purity
"I decree purity over the inner circle, advisors, and cabinet."

9. Decree of Legacy
"I decree that future generations inherit stability, righteousness, and order."

10. Decree of Testimony
"I decree that the testimony of Jesus Christ becomes the spirit of governance in this nation."

PRAYER

*for Nationalisation into the
Kingdom of Heaven*

Scriptural Foundation:

- *John 3:3 – "Jesus answered and said to him, 'Most assuredly, I say to you, unless one is born again, he cannot see the kingdom of God.'"*

- *Philippians 3:20 – "For our citizenship is in heaven, from which we also eagerly wait for the Savior, the Lord Jesus Christ."*

- *Ephesians 2:19 – "Now therefore you are no longer strangers and foreigners, but fellow citizens with the saints and members of the household of God."*

- *Colossians 1:13 – "He has delivered us from the power of darkness and conveyed us into the kingdom of the Son of His love."*

- *Romans 10:9 – "That if you confess with your mouth the Lord Jesus and believe in your heart that God has raised Him from the dead, you will be saved."*

Righteous Judge of Heaven and Earth,

I come before Your throne, the **throne of Grace** in **the Court of Heaven**, in the name of Jesus Christ, my Lord and Saviour. I stand by the power of His precious blood, which has **redeemed me** and **bought my salvation**. I come humbly and boldly, desiring to be **nationalised into the Kingdom of Heaven**—to become a **true citizen of Your heavenly realm.**

Father, Your Word declares in *John 3:3* that **unless one is born again**, they cannot see the Kingdom of God. Today, **I renounce any citizenship** I once held in this world and any **ties to the powers of darkness**. I acknowledge that I have been **transferred from the kingdom of darkness into the Kingdom of the Son** of Your love (*Colossians 1:13*). I declare that I am no longer a stranger or foreigner, but a **fellow citizen with the saints** and a member of the household of God (*Ephesians 2:19*).

Lord Jesus, I believe with all my heart that You are the **Son of the living God**, that You died for my sins and rose again to grant me eternal life (*Romans 10:9*). I now receive You as my **personal Saviour, my Redeemer, the only Way, the Truth**, and **the Life**. You are the **Door to the Father's heart** and the only **path to salvation**. I do not want to **perish** with the world, but to **live eternally with You.**

At this moment, I [Your Full Name] solemnly, sincerely, and truthfully affirm my love, my seriousness, and my desire to follow You and serve You in **holiness and righteousness**. I pledge my full allegiance to You, O King of kings and Lord of lords. I give my loyalty to the third Heaven and honour its **rights and freedoms**. I desire to settle with You, **Lord Jesus**. I repent of the way I have **lived my life and of all my sins**. Take over **my heart and my destiny**. Save me, cleanse me, and change me.

I beseech that You **seal my heavenly citizenship today**. Let the record of **my new identity** be **registered in the Court of Heaven**. Write my name in the **Lamb's Book of Life**, and erase it from the **book of death and judgment**. Let every **legal claim the enemy** has over my past be **cancelled** and **rendered powerless by the blood of Jesus**.

Lord, I am ready to walk the path of **righteousness and holiness**. I cast all **my cares and all of myself upon You**, for You care for me and loved me and laid Your life as the Lamb slain from **the foundation of the world**. Let Your **will be done** in my life as it is in Heaven.

By Your blood, I now receive eternal life. I proclaim that I am a **new creature**. By the word of Your testimony, I am made free indeed. **Fill me and baptize me** with the **Holy Ghost and fire**. Thank You, Lord Jesus, for giving me the right and the power to become a child of God, born **not of flesh but of the Spirit**, according to **the new covenant sealed in Your blood**.

I believe **You died** for me, and on the **third day**, You rose again. You are now seated at the right hand of the **Father in glory**, and I receive You as the Lord of my life. Through You, I have **received grace, peace, forgiveness, and eternal inheritance**. I stand holy, blameless, and without fault before the **Court of Heaven** because of the **righteousness imputed to me through Your sacrifice**.

Now, I **declare that the power of sin, death, and Satan—including the grave**—has been **broken over my life**. I walk in the eternal victory of the Cross. From this day forward, I will never look back. Backward—never. Forward—forever.

Degree and Declare: I am a citizen of Heaven. I live for Your Kingdom. **I walk in Your authority and power**. I receive the **full inheritance of health, peace, righteousness, Wealth, and provision, even eternal life**.

In Jesus' mighty name, I pray.

Amen.

EPILOGUE

When the Daniel President Rises

When this kind of leader takes office, the atmosphere of a nation shifts.

Not by slogan.
Not by spin.
But by spiritual gravity.

A Daniel President does not merely govern he recalibrates a nation's frequency back to heaven's order.

When he rises:

• **Nations stabilise** - because righteous authority becomes a shield around the borders and a compass within the institutions.

• **Righteousness becomes policy** - as integrity moves from private conviction to public architecture.

• **Peace multiplies** - not as a fragile ceasefire, but as the overflow of alignment with divine order.

• **Corruption dies** - because light exposes what darkness cannot defend.

• **Truth rises** - and becomes the operational culture of the government not a slogan, not an aspiration, but a measurable deliverable.

• **People flourish** - because vision replaces fear, clarity replaces confusion, and justice makes room for dignity.

• **Heaven partners with earth** - as the testimony of Jesus becomes the operating system of national leadership.

A Daniel President is not a fantasy.
He is a necessity.
He is the leader the times demand and the kind of governance the world is now bleeding for.

When he rises, empire arrogance breaks.
Demonic principalities lose their foothold.
Generational curses snap.
Nations rediscover their identity.
And the future opens like a scroll.

This is not just political reform this is covenant restoration.

It is the presidency the world needs now. And heaven is already preparing him.

AFTERWORD

When Power Meets Understanding

Every book ends.
Leadership does not.

The final page is not a conclusion; it is a handover. What has been presented here is not theory to admire but an architecture to inhabit. The value of this work will not be measured by agreement, but by **application**.

History is clear on one point: **power without understanding accelerates collapse**. Equally, understanding without authority leaves nations stalled. The future belongs to leaders who integrate both; who carry power with restraint and knowledge with courage.

Daniel did not rule because he was flawless. He ruled because he was **aligned**. He understood the boundaries of authority, the weight of conscience, and the necessity of wisdom beyond himself. He knew when to speak, when to wait, and when to stand immovable; even at personal cost.

That posture remains the differentiator.

The modern presidency sits at the intersection of unprecedented capability and unprecedented fragility. Technology amplifies every decision. Speed compresses deliberation. Public trust is volatile. In such an environment, charisma fades quickly. Only clarity sustains.

This book has argued a simple but demanding truth: **the strength**

of a nation rises or falls with the inner life of its leadership.

Policies can be revised. Systems can be repaired. Economies can be stabilised. But when leadership loses its moral centre, recovery becomes exponentially harder and exponentially more expensive.

The invitation here is not to nostalgia, nor to idealism. It is to **governance maturity;** to lead with eyes open to both visible pressures and invisible realities. To steward authority with humility. To submit power to principle before principle is forced upon power by consequence.

For those who hold office now, this is a moment of recalibration.
For those preparing to lead, this is a blueprint.
For citizens, this is a lens through which to evaluate leadership beyond rhetoric.

The presidency the world needs will not announce itself with noise. It will be recognised by fruit.

Stability where there was chaos.
Justice where there was drift.
Clarity where there was confusion.
Hope where there was fatigue.

When power meets understanding, nations do not merely survive. They **advance**.

The work now moves from page to practice.
The burden transfers to the reader.
The moment remains open.

Govern wisely.

ACKNOWLEDGEMENT

In Stewardship and Gratitude

No work of this nature is produced in isolation.

This book stands at the convergence of conviction, discipline, and obedience to a burden that would not release until it was articulated with clarity. While responsibility for every word rests with the author, gratitude is due to those whose influence, seen and unseen, made this work possible.

First, acknowledgment is given to **God**, the source of wisdom, order, and truth. Leadership begins and ends with Him. Insight is not discovered; it is entrusted. This book exists because divine patterns still speak to human governance, and because heaven continues to offer counsel to those willing to listen.

Gratitude is extended to the **prophets, statesmen, reformers, and thinkers,** named and unnamed, whose lives proved that righteousness and authority are not adversaries. Their testimonies provided both warning and encouragement, reminding us that alignment is costly, but misalignment is catastrophic.

Appreciation is also owed to **leaders in public service**, past and present, who labour under extraordinary pressure with limited margin for error. This book was written with full respect for the weight they carry and the complexity of the environments they navigate. Where this work challenges, it does so in service of strengthening, not condemning, those entrusted with national responsibility.

Special acknowledgment goes to the **next generation of leaders:** students, advisors, civil servants, and emerging policymakers, who refuse to inherit dysfunction as destiny. Your insistence on integrity, clarity, and purpose signals that renewal is not only possible; it is already underway.

Finally, gratitude is offered for the **discipline of obedience;** the quiet hours of writing, refining, and aligning thought with truth. This book demanded patience, precision, and restraint. It was shaped not for applause, but for impact.

If these pages contribute in any measure to steadier leadership, clearer governance, and nations better aligned with justice and truth, then their purpose has been fulfilled.

May this work serve as a tool, a mirror, and a reminder: that leadership is a trust, that power answers to order, and that the future belongs to those who govern with understanding.

With humility and resolve.

ABOUT THE AUTHOR

Anthony Mwangi — The Branch Seated In Zion

Anthony Mwangi is a prophetic teacher, strategist, and author whose work operates at the intersection of spiritual intelligence, governance architecture, and leadership formation. He is known for articulating complex truths with executive clarity; translating ancient patterns into modern systems capable of sustaining nations, institutions, and leaders under pressure.

Rooted in Scripture and disciplined by order, his writings advance a singular thesis: alignment precedes authority, and authority determines outcomes. Anthony approaches leadership not as performance, but as stewardship, where conscience is a core competency and wisdom is the primary asset.

His prophetic framework integrates multidimensional insight across spirit, soul, body, time, and structure, offering leaders tools for discernment, decision-making, and legacy construction. This methodology has informed teachings, books, and leadership materials designed to restore clarity where power has outpaced understanding.

The President — The Man the World Needs Now reflects his commitment to truth without dilution and governance without theatrics. It is written for leaders who recognise that the future will not be stabilised by louder voices, but by deeper alignment.

Anthony writes with one objective: to see leaders govern with integrity, nations recover their moral centre, and authority return to its original design; accountable, purposeful, and enduring.

He remains focused on producing work that strengthens institutions, equips the next generation, and leaves a testimony measured not by reach but by fruit.

BOOKS BY THIS AUTHOR

The True Church (Ekklesia): The Undisputed Government Of Heaven On Earth (Undiluted Truth Christian Books)

The Church was never designed to be a passive audience. It was crafted to be a governing body; Heaven's operational command centre on the earth.

This prophetic masterpiece unveils the Church in her original mandate: a ruling, legislative, fire-crowned government seated in Christ, built to administer righteousness, execute divine justice, and steward the expansion of the Kingdom with unshakeable authority.

Moving beyond institutional religion, this book repositions the reader inside the architectural blueprint of God's eternal design, where the Ekklesia stands as Heaven's governing senate, the Lamb's undefeated Heavyweight Government operating in light, truth, and dominion.

Each chapter pulls you deeper into the designer realm of the Word, where identity becomes structure and revelation becomes strategy. You will discover:

The true governmental nature of the Church
How sons legislate from Zion through rest, not striving
Why hell cannot contend with a people aligned to the Throne

How the 7-Dimensional Word of God equips believers for rule
The rise of Kingdom coalitions, watchtowers, and councils
The architecture of divine order that establishes peace without end
This is not just a teaching; it is a governmental activation. A call to rise, build, legislate, and stand in your ordained post within Heaven's expanding Kingdom.

For reformers, intercessors, apostolic builders, prophetic architects, and every believer hungry to move beyond survival into governance, this book is your blueprint.

Step into the council.
Stand in the light.
Take your seat in the Undisputed Government of the Lamb.

The Armour Of Light: Unlocking The Mystery Of Divine Warfare (Undiluted Truth Christian Books)

In the last days, the battlefield is no longer fought with swords and spears, but with light, truth, and the Spirit. The Armour of Light: Unlocking the Mystery of Divine Warfare is a prophetic unveiling of God's end-time strategy for His chosen remnant.

This masterpiece reveals the hidden dimensions of the Word of God and the power of the Holy Spirit as the true armour that clothes, protects, and empowers the believer. Through spiritology, soulogy, physiology, and theology, the mystery of warfare is unfolded—showing how the Sabbath is God's dwelling place, the Courtroom of Heaven is His battlefield, and the Bride is His warrior.

Drawing from ancient truths and prophetic revelations, Anthony Mwangi — the BRANCH seated in Zion — uncovers the role of man in God's eternal judgment, the secret of Christ's blood as the light of warfare, and the revelation of the 7-dimensional Word as the weapon that disarms the dragon, the beast, and the false prophet.

This book is not just a teaching, but a weapon in itself. It equips the end-time believer to stand clothed in fire, sealed by the Spirit, and ready to triumph in the last battle.

If you are called to be part of the remnant, this is your manual of divine warfare.

Sabbath: The Name Of The Holy Spirit — God's Covenant Protocol For The Last Days

This book unveils a groundbreaking revelation: the Sabbath is the Name, Seal, and Rest of the Holy Spirit, and the end-time Church cannot walk in covenant power without understanding this identity. Drawing from the 7-Dimensional Word of God, this work decodes the Sabbath as God's ancient–future protocol — the original sign of His presence, the governing code of His kingdom, and the prophetic mark that distinguishes His remnant in the last days.

You will discover how the Sabbath reveals God's hidden Name, aligns the mind with divine order, and positions the body as the dwelling place where the Spirit rests. From Eden's first seventh-day revelation to the sealed remnant of Revelation, this book demonstrates that to hallow the Sabbath is to hallow His Name, and that the restoration of Sabbath order is the restoration of God's government on earth.

Packed with visionary insights, prophetic typology, and a full blueprint for spiritual formation, this book equips believers to:

Understand the Sabbath as the signature identity of the Holy Spirit

Discern the covenant seal that separates truth from deception in the last days

Rebuild the altar of rest in the mind, heart, and body

Walk in the rhythm, protection, and judgment of God's kingdom order

Stand in Zion as those who have entered His Rest

This is not merely theology — it is kingdom strategy.
A call to return.
A summons to alignment.
A preparation for the remnant.

SABBATH: The Name of the Holy Spirit is your guide to reclaiming God's original covenant protocol, and stepping into the Rest that marks His people for the final generation.

The Issue Of The Horse: The Courtroom Indictment Against Easter, Christmas, And Modern Pagan Feasts (Undiluted Truth Christian Books)

In a generation reshaped by convenience, tradition, and cultural drift, what if the greatest spiritual compromise is hiding in plain sight?

This book issues a bold, courtroom-level challenge to the most celebrated religious holidays: Easter, Christmas, and the modern feasts that carry the fingerprints of Babylon more than the signature of God.

Drawing from prophetic insight, forensic Scripture analysis, and the ancient protocols of the Holy Spirit, The Issue of the Horse unmasks the systems that led believers away from covenant identity and into ritual mixtures dressed as worship. It reveals how syncretism infiltrated the church, how altars were exchanged, and why heaven's court is calling for a return to purity.

This is not a rant. It's a verdict.
A clear, uncompromising case built line upon line—rooted in the King James Bible, reinforced by historical evidence, and charged with a future-focused mandate: to realign the body of Christ with the original statutes of the Spirit.

Readers will discover:

The prophetic meaning of "the horse" and how it exposes counterfeit worship

Why certain feasts carry a spiritual indictment

How the courtroom of heaven evaluates worship, sacrifice, and alignment

The clash between the Holy Spirit's Sabbath identity and modern religious tradition

The call of Zion for believers to return to covenant rest and Spirit-governed truth

This book is a wake-up call for believers, leaders, intercessors, and truth-seekers who know something is off but have lacked the language, evidence, and prophetic clarity to name it.

If you're ready to confront the mixture, reclaim ancient order, and stand in the firelight of truth, step into the courtroom.
The Spirit has issued a summons.
The verdict is unfolding.
And the remnant is rising.

Stars From The East (Irathiro)

From the snows of Mount Kenya to the throne of eternal fire, The Scroll of Irathiro unveils a prophetic revelation hidden for generations. This masterpiece carries the light of divine remembrance — a message to restore identity, awaken the remnant, and call nations back to covenant truth.

Through the 7-Dimensional Word of God and the Spirit's rhythm of revelation, the author unfolds mysteries connecting ancient prophecy, African identity, and the returning glory of Christ — the King whose hair is white as wool and whose eyes burn with eternal purpose.

Each chapter breathes with vision and fire: from the golden offerings of the Magi to the judgment of nations, from the altar of Zion to the rivers of counsel flowing from the throne. It is not merely a book — it is a scroll of destiny, written in light and sealed in blood.

Those who read will find themselves within the story of restoration — called to stand as witnesses in the Court of Heaven, bearing the sign of the covenant and the song of the East.

Prophetic. Powerful. Undiluted truth.
This is not history retold — it is prophecy fulfilled.

Deliverance By Fire: Unlocking The Courts, Thrones, And Altars Of True Freedom (Undiluted Truth Christian Books)

This prophetic manual is not just a teaching — it is a spiritual courtroom, an altar of judgment, and a throne of fire. Deliverance by Fire unveils the divine order of freedom as legislated in heaven's courts and manifested through the Spirit of Truth on earth.

Within these pages, you will encounter the architecture of true deliverance:
the Courts of Heaven, where accusations are silenced;
the Thrones of Dominion, where believers reign in Christ;
and the Altars of Fire, where covenants are purified and destinies reborn.

Built upon the revelation of the Seven Spirits of God, this book exposes the counterfeit thrones of darkness — and trains the sons and daughters of Zion to war by decree, not emotion; by the Word, not the flesh. Each chapter blends courtroom insight, prophetic instruction, and altar-based declarations to forge warriors of holiness and rest.

Through this 7-dimensional model — Spiritology, Soulogy, Physiology, Theology, Chronology, Typology, and Technology — Anthony Mwangi reveals how the Spirit of Judgment and Burning restores divine order, purges bloodlines, and reclaims the altars of families, cities, and nations.

This book will teach you to:

Minister deliverance through heavenly legal protocol.

Break bloodline covenants and generational curses with the fire of truth.

Build Sabbath altars that sustain freedom and spiritual authority.

Operate in the courts of Zion, where Christ is both Judge and Advocate.

Move from manifestation to dominion — from reaction to legislation.

Deliverance by Fire is more than deliverance — it is reformation. It is the blueprint of how heaven reclaims the earth through purified vessels who have become living stones and burning altars of the Spirit.

When you finish reading, you will not just understand deliverance — you will embody it.

The Marriage Supper Of The Lamb: The Final War Of Love (Undiluted Truth Christian Books)

In this groundbreaking prophetic work, The Marriage Supper of the Lamb: The Final War of Love, Anthony Mwangi unveils the hidden architecture of the end-time covenant between Christ and His Bride. More than a celebration, the Marriage Supper is revealed as Heaven's ultimate act of war — where intimacy becomes victory and union becomes dominion.

Drawing from the 7-Dimensional Word of God, the 3 Modes of Revelation, and a detailed study of 18 biblical marriages + 7 prophetic weddings, this book exposes God's protocol for the last days: how the Lamb wins by sacrifice, how the Lion reigns by fire, and how the Bride rises to rule with Him in eternal covenant.

Readers will discover:

The divine protocol behind all revelation — precept upon precept, line upon line

Why the Marriage Supper is an ordered decree of judgment, glory, and love

The supernatural patterns behind biblical unions and how they reveal Christ's final victory

The role of the Bride in the end-time war of worship, fire, purity, and rest

How Heaven structures intimacy, government, and dominion

The mystery of the Lamb and the Lion in the same Christ

The prophetic meaning of garments, oil, trumpets, tables, crowns, and sceptres

What it truly means to sit at the King's table at the end of the age

With poetic revelation and airtight prophetic logic, Mwangi guides the reader step-by-step — from Genesis unions to Revelation's wedding — unveiling how every covenant, sacrifice, feast, and throne room moment points toward one climactic event: the eternal joining of the Lamb and His Bride in the Final War of Love.

Whether you are a pastor, intercessor, theologian, prophetic teacher, or hungry believer, this book will transform your understanding of the end times, awaken your identity as the Bride, and align you with Heaven's strategy for the last battle.

The table is set.
The sceptre is extended.
The crown is prepared.
The Bride is rising.

Step into the revelation. Step into the war. Step into the Supper.

The Message From Jesus Christ Return: Return, O Israel (Undiluted Truth Christian Books)

A Prophetic Warning. A Heavenly Invitation. A Call to the Remnant.

The Message from Jesus Christ: RETURN, O ISRAEL is not merely a book; it is a divine summons. Delivered through The Lord Jesus Christ Himself, given scripture, revelation, and the voice of the Spirit, this work carries a message the Lord Jesus Christ is giving to this generation: Return. Awaken. Prepare.

Across powerful precepts drawn directly from the Word of God, this book unveils the urgency of Christ's soon coming, the restoration of Israel's true spiritual identity, and the gathering of God's scattered sons from every nation. From Isaiah to Zephaniah, Ezekiel to Matthew, each passage is opened through a prophetic lens using the 3M (spoken, written, vision) + 7D model — a unique Spirit-breathed method for interpreting scripture in these last days.

The message is clear:
The King is at the door. The nations tremble. The churches must awaken. And Israel must return to her God.

You will discover:

The true meaning of the Great Day of the LORD

Why God is calling His remnant out of the nations

The spiritual identity and awakening of Israel in our time

How Christ Himself is summoning His people through scripture

The prophetic significance of the present generation

How to stand ready for the Second Coming with purity and understanding

More than a warning, this is an invitation — from Jesus Christ Himself — to come out of confusion, return to covenant identity, and align with heaven's final movement.

Whether you are a believer seeking clarity, a watchman longing to understand the times, or a seeker drawn by the Spirit, this book will stir your soul, awaken your spirit, and ignite a deeper devotion to the King of Kings.

The Spirit and the Bride say, Come.
Even so, Lord Jesus, come quickly.